Living with
the Old Testament

KAREN A. HAMILTON

NOVALIS

© 2012 Novalis Publishing Inc.

Cover design and layout: Audrey Wells
Cover artwork: Sarah Hall (www.sarahhallstudio.com)

Interior images: Eyewire: p. 4; W.P. Wittman: pp. 9, 21; Plaisted: pp. 11, 25, 31, 32; Fotosearch: p. 17; Jupiter Images: p. 29

Published by Novalis

Publishing Office
10 Lower Spadina Avenue, Suite 400
Toronto, Ontario, Canada
M5V 2Z2

Head Office
4475 Frontenac Street
Montréal, Québec, Canada
H2H 2S2

www.novalis.ca

ISBN: 978-2-89646-414-2

Cataloguing in Publication is available from Library and Archives Canada.

Printed in Canada.

We acknowledge the financial support of the Government of Canada through the Canada Book Fund for business development activities.

5 4 3 2 1   16 15 14 13 12

1 What is the Old Testament and why should we read it?

The Old Testament is essential reading for Christians. Reading this collection of ancient Scriptures, hearing them proclaimed at church, studying them and praying with them reveal God to us. They help us to continue to discover and experience God's relationship with us and with creation.

The Old Testament tells us who God is and why God creates. More specifically, it tells us how God relates to us and what kind of people God wants us to be. It describes the ways we make mistakes and hurt each other, and reminds us that God loves us in spite of ourselves. God continually calls us back into a loving, just and fair relationship. The Old Testament is about life; it emphasizes that how we live our lives matters. These sacred Scriptures teach us about leadership, justice, peace, righteousness, mercy, grace, prayer, relationship and faithfulness to God and to each other.

Through the many books of the Old Testament, we learn about God's covenant with us and God's vital, active presence in the world. God created us and loves us, and for that reason desires to be in relationship with us. God promises to hold us close and gives us guidelines for living faithfully in that relationship. We hear of God's relationship of promise with all of humanity right from the beginning, and then God's promise to Abraham to ensure life and descendants, who would become the Jewish people. Our ancestors in the faith – Moses, Abraham, Sarah, David and countless others – promised to be faithful, but when they strayed from their promises, God, in love and justice, kept calling them back into an intimate relationship. The Old Testament shows us in living colour that not only is God a God of love and justice, but God is also persistent!

Moses leads the Israelites to freedom

As Christians, we believe that through Jesus Christ we are now a part of that ongoing relationship of promise. Thankfully, God is just as persistent with us.

The Old Testament talks about the big questions of life:

- What is our responsibility towards creation?
- How are we to show justice and mercy to others?

- What does true leadership look like?
- What should we do when we are angry or in despair?
- Why do we hurt others?

The Old Testament also talks about the big questions of faith:

- How does hurting others harm our relationship with God?
- What are the consequences of not living as God asks?
- Are there rewards for following God's laws?
- What is true repentance?
- Why does God call us to be peacemakers?
- What does it mean to live in the grace of God?
- Does God cause bad things to happen to good people?
- How is what we do in our daily lives supposed to reflect God?
- How do we live faithfully, both when times are tough and when times are good?
- How and why should we praise God?

Reading the Old Testament not only deepens our faith and our relationship with God, making us more aware of the complexity and mystery of the divine, but also gives us specific, concrete guidelines for how to live our everyday lives. It helps us to reflect on our life and faith and to move forward as we begin to answer the complex questions listed above. Reading the Old Testament makes us think. It introduces us to a wide variety of people and situations that have a lot in common with what we are facing in our own lives and context. It does not shy away from telling stories of anger, violence, battle, lust, power, greed and hatred. These were realities in the times in which the Old Testament books were written, and they are realities now. Delving into the Old Testament helps us learn how these tendencies lead us away from God. We also find numerous stories of faithfulness, courage, love, hope and humility. These stories are a source of strength and inspiration when we are struggling in some way.

The Old Testament has been considered profoundly important for Christians since the very beginning of our tradition. That is why the Lectionary (the pattern of Scripture readings to be proclaimed in the liturgy) contains an Old Testament passage every Sunday, except during the Easter season, when there is a reading from the Acts of the Apostles (from the New Testament) instead. Most Sundays of the year also feature an Old Testament Psalm.

The Old Testament can at times seem long, hard to understand, irrelevant or even boring. But who ever said reading Scripture would be easy and comforting all the time? If it ever stops being challenging, we have probably missed the point of the passage we are reading. And that includes the texts we think we understand perfectly, such as the 23rd Psalm!

2 When and why were the various books written?

Written sources of the Old Testament likely began to be assembled in the time of King David, around a thousand years before the birth of Christ. The people of Israel were starting to see themselves as a distinct people with a land of their own, a unique identity and a particular relationship to their God; gathering their sacred writings was a way to strengthen that identity and preserve their faith stories for future generations. Some Old Testament books are said to be written by certain authors, but there were likely a variety of sources.

The Old Testament took on much of the shape that we have now during the time of the Exile (587–538 BC), when the people of Israel were captives in Babylon after the Babylonians invaded their land and destroyed the holy Temple in Jerusalem in 586 BC. This terrible and painful era for the people of Israel is reflected in the Old Testament, revealing their understanding of their relationship to God in tragic and changed times.

Much of the compilation of the Old Testament happened after the people returned from Exile to the land of Israel. They were struggling to adjust to new and difficult circumstances with different threatening powers in the area. The Old Testament was finalized a few centuries after the time of Jesus, when the Roman Empire had completely destroyed the city of Jerusalem and the Temple for a second time and the people had to find their way forward in faith in very changed circumstances once more.

Knowing the outline of the story of the people of Israel, our ancestors in the faith, helps us understand both why evil and destruction are so thoroughly acknowledged in the Old Testament and why the sovereignty of God over all the earth is such a profound statement of faith.

The Old Testament is the collection of Scriptures that Jesus knew and used extensively in his preaching and teaching. These are the Scriptures that the apostles and early Church knew and used long before the New Testament was broadly accepted or even written.

③ How are the Old Testament and New Testament connected?

As Christians, we follow Jesus Christ as our Lord and Saviour and believe that in Jesus and through the power of the Holy Spirit, we see and experience God the Father.

Jesus was a Jew. Mary and Joseph were Jewish parents who brought their son up in the practices and faith of the Jewish people. Jesus prayed in the Temple in Jerusalem, the physical centre of Judaism at that time; he also prayed and read and spoke in the synagogue in Nazareth, where he grew up. He never denied Judaism as a faith and a way of life. In fact, he said that he came "not to destroy the [Jewish] law but to fulfill it" (Matthew 5:17).

Jesus teaching in the Temple

For both Jews and Christians, what Christians call the Old Testament is a witness to and revelation of God. God's covenant relationship with the Jews, the people of Jesus, which is attested to in the Old Testament, can stand side by side with God's covenant relationship with Christians in the name and peace of Our Lord Jesus Christ, which is rooted in the Old Testament and witnessed to in the New Testament. There is nothing in our proper understanding of the Old or New Testaments that encourages or allows anti-Semitism.

The New Testament quotes or alludes to many Old Testament figures or passages; it is obvious that the various authors of the New Testament were both deeply familiar with the Old Testament and believed in its essential place in the life of the believer in Christ. The books of the prophet Isaiah and the Psalms are quoted or referred to in the New Testament most often, but King David, Jonah and lesser-known figures such as Melchizedek also appear.

The Old Testament does not explicitly predict the birth of Jesus, but clearly reveals that the Incarnation is in line with God's way of relating to us. Texts such as Isaiah 7 and 9 and the Suffering Servant passages (Isaiah 42:1-4, 49:1-6, 50:4-9 and 52:13-53) are key to the Christian understanding of Jesus as Messiah. The following passage is proclaimed on Good Friday, for example:

> See, my servant shall prosper; he shall be exalted and lifted up, and shall be very high.
> Just as there were many who were astonished at him—
> so marred was his appearance, beyond human semblance, and his form beyond that of mortals—

Jonah in the belly of the whale

so he shall startle many nations;
kings shall shut their mouths because of him;
for that which had not been told them they shall see,
and that which they had not heard they shall contemplate.
(Isaiah 52:13-15)

4 Which Bible translation is best?

There are many English translations of the Bible to choose from, but some are more faithful than others to the original texts. The New Revised Standard Version (NRSV) is recognized as being an excellent balance of scholarly translation of the biblical languages combined with a poetic, accessible use of language. This is the version commonly used in worship in Canadian churches today.

5 Why does the Old Testament seem so complicated?

The Old Testament is more than two thirds of what Christians call the Bible. It is made up of many different books, in many different styles of writing, written over many different time periods. We find stories, epic narratives, poetry, prophecy, songs, dreams, instructions, descriptions, records, genealogies, myths and history. This variety of material can sometimes make the text hard to understand and interpret. It is complicated, just as our lives, humanity and historical realities are complicated. The variety in the Old Testament gives us countless ways to see the depth and breadth of God's activity in our lives and in the world.

The Old Testament also contains conversations and arguments that people – including Adam and Eve; Abraham, Sarah and Hagar; and Moses – have with God, as well as God's response, which sometimes includes the changing of the divine mind. The Old Testament communicates both the ideals of sacred worship and the human, homely details of life – what people wore and ate, their customs, and how they related to each other and to God. It sets out words and actions of prophets and kings, describes the Jewish people's journey to a land of their own through what was (and still is) a troubled part of the world, and reports the decisions and circumstances that saved or harmed life.

Here is a summary of the books of the Old Testament, organized according to its main categories, along with their overall message.

Old Testament books	Overall message
Pentateuch	
Genesis, Exodus, Leviticus, Numbers and Deuteronomy	The Pentateuch outlines God's actions of grace and subsequent instructions for living life in faithful relationship to God and to others.

→

Old Testament books	Overall message
Historical Books	
Joshua, Judges, Ruth, 1 & 2 Samuel, 1 & 2 Kings, 1 & 2 Chronicles, Ezra, Nehemiah, *Tobit*,* *Judith*,* Esther, and *1 & 2 Maccabees**	The Historical Books offer us great detail as the people of Israel strive to come together from their tribes and form a nation, with both faithful and unfaithful actions. Lots of things go right and lots of things go wrong. Much violence and struggle are recorded, but also much faithfulness.
Wisdom Literature	
Job	The book of Job deals with the big question of whether God causes bad things to happen to good people. (The entire OT wrestles with this question, but it is particularly focused in Job.) Job's question is our question still.
Psalms	The 150 Psalms offer 150 ways of describing in poetry the complexities of human life – the joys, challenges, fears and praise that people bring before God.
Proverbs	Proverbs are concrete pieces of advice for how to live in relationship to God and others in ways that are fair, reasonable, successful and faithful.

* Books in italics are part of the Catholic canon (official list of books) but not the Protestant canon.

Old Testament books	Overall message
Wisdom Literature (cont'd)	
Ecclesiastes	Ecclesiastes is a poetic book that speaks theologically about human efforts to control their lives and understand a complicated world.
Song of Solomon	This book is a poetic, colourful description of human love that has sometimes been used to describe the love between God and humanity.
*Wisdom of Solomon**	This book speaks of how the power of divine wisdom is at work in human history.
*Sirach**	The teacher Ben Sira is a useful guide to Judaism and to the world of Jesus and the early Christians.
Prophetic Literature	
Isaiah, Jeremiah, Lamentations, *Baruch,** Ezekiel, Daniel, Hosea, Joel, Amos, Obadiah, Jonah, Micah, Nahum, Habakkuk, Zephaniah, Haggai, Zechariah, Malachi	The prophets challenge the people when they need to be challenged and comfort them when they need to be comforted. Prophets call people forward into a vision of God's justice and peace enacted on earth. Christians see the final prophet, Malachi (whose name means "my messenger"), as calling us forward into the reality of God's incarnation in Jesus Christ.

* Books in italics are part of the Catholic canon (official list of books) but not the Protestant canon.

What is biblical prophecy?

Biblical prophecy is never fortune-telling, but rather is a message about what will happen if people continue to stray from God. Prophets warn about the consequences of acting unjustly, but always hold out the possibility of right relations with God being restored if the people repent and turn their behaviour in a new, more faithful direction.

6 Do all Christian bibles contain the same Old Testament books?

Catholic and Protestant Old Testaments differ in their number of books. For Protestants, the Old Testament contains 39 books; for Catholics, it contains 46 books. While the first five books of the Bible (the Pentateuch) are identical in both traditions, the Catholic canon contains the following additional books: Tobit, Judith, additions to Esther, and 1 and 2 Maccabees (Historical Books); Wisdom of Solomon and Sirach (Wisdom Literature); and Baruch, plus additions to Daniel (Prophetic Literature). These books are from the Greek version of the Old Testament, called the Septuagint, rather than the Hebrew version, called the Tanakh.

A scroll containing the Jewish Scriptures

⑦ Why is there is so much violence in the Old Testament?

Reading, understanding and interpreting violent passages in the Old Testament – such as Exodus 23:23-33 and Psalms 3:7, 137:9 and 143:12 – is a challenge. We are often overwhelmed by the violence in our lives and world; why would we want to read about it in the Old Testament? But that is exactly the point. These difficult texts serve as a mirror that reflects our own lives and behaviour, or as a challenge leading us to renewed faith and justice. (Sometimes the texts do both at the same time.) The violence we read about and hear about in the Old Testament has the same roots and causes as the violence of our day – power, hatred, control, lust, greed, fear, jealousy, misunderstanding. This violence caused pain, injustice, destruction and death in ancient times, just as it does in our day. When we read the Old Testament as a whole, we realize that violence was not God's will then and is not God's will now.

But what about those passages that speak of God calling for violence against a people other than the Israelites? These kinds of passages are deeply troubling; some people find it hard to believe in such a God.

There is no easy answer, but we believe that the Bible speaks about all of human life: its joys and challenges, its faithfulness and unfaithfulness, its experience of truth but also, in its freedom, its possibility of misinterpretation. The movement of understanding through the Old Testament reveals God as the God of all people and all places. God is gracious and merciful to all people. God calls all people, even those who do not know him (see Isaiah 45:1, where Cyrus the Persian is anointed by God) into divine service. This witnesses to the truth that the interpretation of God promoting violence against a particular people in a particular time and place was and is incorrect.

Violence is found in the New Testament, as well. It is completely false to refer to "the God of the Old Testament" as a God of violence and "the God of the New Testament" as a God of peace. This position was rejected by the early Church as heretical in the second century. The same God is revealed in both Scriptures.

We must see Scripture as an interrelated whole, and not simply as separate pieces of text. Individual verses and short phrases can become lines of communication that open us to God, but should never be used to support a narrow argument or to justify hurting other people.

8 Why is the land so important to the people of Israel?

The Old Testament speaks of the ancient land of Israel as a gift from God to God's people. For many of our Jewish sisters and brothers today, this idea is still very important to their faith and self-understanding. This can be a difficult concept for Christians. While we believe that God became incarnate in Jesus in a particular time and in a particular land, our faith has a universal understanding that does not tie it in the same way to the land of Israel or any other land.

9 How should I read the Old Testament?

Modern biblical scholarship and archaeology have taught us many helpful things about the background and details of the Old Testament writings and peoples, but the amount of information can be intimidating. There are so many books out there. If our main exposure to the Old Testament Scriptures is hearing them at church, there is a complication: while the lectionary often provides Gospel passages in the sequence in which they appear in the Bible, passages from the Old Testament are matched with Gospel readings in ways that often break up the epic narratives or jump around from prophet to prophet. This approach makes it hard for us to get a good sense of any particular Old Testament book or author. The two epic narratives that do make it into the lectionary – the stories of the Exodus and King David, which are key stories of our faith – appear in the summer months in the northern hemisphere, when many people are away.

When listening to an Old Testament passage at church or reading on your own, remember that as holy Scripture, the Old Testament is God's story and our story. Then sit back and take in the reading! Develop an ear for the ancient style of making a point, which involves repetition; notice the long lists of names, which signify relationship and continuity in the faith story; listen for details about the decoration of the Temple in Jerusalem; spend time with vibrant characters who seem larger than life in both their courage and their failures. Even sections that seem at first to be only about history or politics connect God, the people and creation. Delight in the comic moments as well, for God indeed has a sense of humour! Ask yourself what God is saying to you in these texts, but do not expect an immediate answer. Reading the Old Testament is a journey with the questions of life and faith for our whole existence. Savour the experience and let the words take root in your heart.

10 Why should I begin "In the beginning..."?

To start a pattern of personal Old Testament reading, begin at the beginning, with the "In the beginning" words of Genesis, chapter 1, verse 1. Try to read a chapter a day. It will take you years to read the whole Old Testament this way, but you will be richly blessed. By immersing yourself in the stories of the people and situations of the Old Testament on a regular basis, you will come to feel the vibrancy of God's faithful, loving presence in your life. Knowing that these characters, with all their strengths and weaknesses, could be instruments of God's reign helps us remember that we can be God's instruments, too. If a particular chapter or book is confusing, move on to another section, but first pause and ask yourself why the writers and editors who gathered the biblical texts together felt that our ancestors in the faith and we, their descendants, needed to hear that passage.

11 What does the Old Testament have to do with me today?

The Old Testament is a treasure trove of wisdom, guidance, love and hope in God, and is as relevant in the third millennium as it ever was. A glance at just a few chapters of these rich and thought-provoking Scriptures helps to highlight key faith moments that continue to shape us today.

Genesis 21: "Sarah conceived and bore Abraham a son…"

This chapter of the first book of the Old Testament is a wonderful example of the vibrant relationship God had with our early ancestors in faith. The promised son Isaac, whose presence will ensure the inheritance and blessing of this family, is about to be born to Abraham and Sarah. Although they had tried hard to believe God's promise that they would one day have a son, and that their descendants would be as numerous as the stars in the sky, Abraham and Sarah began to doubt as the years passed and the couple became elderly. Wanting to take control of their lives, Abraham had a son by the slave woman Hagar. Now, faced with the fulfillment of God's promise, Abraham fails again, sending Hagar and her son Ishmael out into the desert to die so Ishmael will not be a threat to Isaac's inheritance.

What happened next was startling. God showed up! God spoke to Hagar and promised that her son, too, would be the ancestor of a great nation. God is not limited by Abraham and Sarah, or by the constraints of human understanding. Ishmael is considered the ancestor of Muslims, while Isaac is considered the ancestor of Jews and Christians. In this way the three great monotheistic religions share a common ancestor: Abraham. We are truly brothers and sisters in faith.

Reflection question:

- What would happen if we really believed and acted in the belief that God uses whom God chooses and is vibrantly present in the lives of those who seem to be outsiders to us?

Exodus 34: "The Lord said, 'I hereby make a covenant.'"

This is the second of three versions of the Ten Commandments. (The other two are found in Exodus 20 and Deuteronomy 5.) God has, in a tremendous act of grace, freed the people of Israel from slavery in Egypt and is leading them through the wilderness back to the land of Israel. After such an act of love and grace, God gives Moses and the people a guide or instruction manual to just and right living, to fair and faithful relationship with God and with each other. No sooner do the people receive this tremendous gift of the Ten Commandments than they turn to other gods and seek reassurance in a difficult time. God is angry at their lack of faith in the God of Israel, but Moses serves as a mediator between the people and God, and the gift of grace in guidelines for right living is reissued.

Moses receives the Ten Commandments

Leviticus 24: "I am the Lord your God."

This is one of many chapters in Leviticus that are full of at times mind-numbing lists or details. This Old Testament book deals in an exhaustive way with the issues of sacrifice (which was a way of acknowledging the supremacy of God or restoring oneself to right relationship with God), priesthood, disease, festivals, the furnishings of the tabernacle and the care of the land. The point is that the details of our lives matter, and God relates to life in all its aspects. The Bible never advocates a hard-and-fast distinction between physical things and things of the spirit.

Numbers 11: "The people complained in the hearing of the Lord..."

The people are still wandering in the desert, learning how they are to govern their lives in a way that shows the reality and vibrant interaction of God. Life in the desert is tough. No matter how bad slavery in Egypt was, human memory can be short. The people start to complain and long for their old life. Moses, as their leader, is overwhelmed, and clearly expresses his feelings to God. God responds with a model for leadership. Moses does not have to bear the responsibility alone, but can appoint 70 elders to share it with him. The journey and the caring for the people can continue.

Reflection question:

- How do we understand, support and nurture Christian leadership in and for our world today? How do you show Christian leadership in your family, community or workplace?

Deuteronomy 8: "Take care that you do not forget the Lord your God…"

The decades of wandering in the desert wilderness are nearly over. Moses restates the deep truths of God's instructions in a way that the people can understand. He reminds them how easy it is, when we are comfortable and affluent, to give priority to material possessions rather than to God.

Reflection question:

- What are your priorities? How would someone who knows you see that God is the most important reality in your life?

1 Kings 3: "Solomon loved the Lord…"

Solomon, son of David, is king of Israel. This complex man is known for his tremendous wisdom, for his vast number of wives and concubines and, later in the biblical narrative, for some cruel policies that result in the kingdom of Israel being divided into two. Solomon, like us, is human. In this chapter, Solomon realizes that wisdom is worth far more than long life, riches or security from those who would oppose him.

Reflection question:

• What joyful or painful experiences in your life have helped you grow in wisdom? Have you sensed God near to you at these moments? How?

Job 38: "The Lord said, 'I will question you, and you shall declare to me.'"

The book of Job wrestles for 42 chapters with a searing question of our time: Why do bad things happen to good people? In this chapter, God reminds Job of the divine mystery and power that cannot be contained even by our human questions. God also says clearly that, contrary to the belief of Job's "friends," the terrible things that can happen in life do not come to us as retribution or punishment. God walks with us through our darkest days and nights.

Reflection question:

• How do you find the strength to engage with and stay faithful to God in tough times?

Proverbs 15: "A glad heart makes a cheerful countenance…"

Proverbs is a witty book of brief, practical proverbs for living in a way that is faithful, just, well-mannered, shrewd, wise and abounding in common sense. God is in the details, indeed; this book reminds us that we are not to try and force an artificial separation between what might be called "spiritual" and what might be called "physical" in this life. It all belongs to God.

Reflection question:
- What would the world look like if we took more seriously the biblical witness that every part of life belongs to God?

Isaiah 49:16: "See, I have inscribed you on the palms of my hands…"

It is said that the prophets comfort the afflicted and afflict the comfortable. These spokespersons for God convey God's word of love and challenge to certain people and situations, as the need arises.

When the people are living lives of comfort and ignoring the needs of the poor and vulnerable, the prophets speak harshly. When the people are suffering in Exile, after much of what they held dear has been destroyed, the prophets speak of hope and returning home. Both messages are always given in the context of God's great message – God loves us intimately and abundantly.

God loves us truly and deeply, and in that love calls us to love others truly and deeply as well. Thanks be to God!

Reflection question:

Who are the prophets in our world and in our faith communities – those who challenge us to justice and remind us that God loves us and all people? Pray for their strength.

12 Where can I learn more about the Old Testament?

Here are some excellent resources to help you explore the Old Testament in more depth:

Living with the Psalms. Karen A. Hamilton. Toronto: Novalis, 2011.

The Acceptable Year of the Lord: Preaching the Old Testament with Faith, Finesse and Fervour. Karen A. Hamilton. Ottawa: Novalis, 2008.

The New Jerome Biblical Commentary. Raymond Brown, Joseph Fitzmyer, and Roland Murphy (eds.). 3rd edition. Toronto: Novalis, 2011.

The New Oxford Annotated Bible (New Revised Standard Version). Fourth edition. Michael D. Coogan (ed.). Toronto: Oxford University Press, 2010.

The Old Testament: A Very Short Introduction. Michael D. Coogan. Toronto: Oxford University Press, 2008.

Theology of the Old Testament. Walter Brueggemann. Minneapolis, MN: Fortress Press, 2005.